Chakra Divination Ultimate Balance Journal

Melissa Alvarez

Adrema Press

A NOTICE TO THE READER

The ideas and suggestions contained in the Chakra Divination books are the opinion of the author based on her own experiences and are not intended as a substitute for psychological counseling or consultation with your physician. This book is not a medical guide. All medical references are intended to show the relationship between the body and the chakras, not as advice for medical problems or conditions. All matters regarding your health require medical supervision by a licensed doctor. The author and publisher assume no liability or responsibility for your actions or damages resulting from this books information or use of the journal.

Text Copyright © 2010 by Melissa Alvarez
Chakra Card Designs, Chakra Chart Designs and Chakra Divination Card Meanings Copyright © 2010 by Melissa Alvarez All Rights Reserved.
All artwork is copyrighted by the artist and may not be reproduced by any means, electronic or otherwise.
Author Websites: www.MelissaAlvarez.com and www.APsychicHaven.com

ISBN: 1-59611-047-3
ISBN 13: 978-1-59611-047-2

All Rights Reserved. No part of this Divination method, including cards and charts, may be reproduced by any method whatsoever. Except for use in any review, the reproduction or utilization of this work in whole or in part in any form by any electronic, mechanical or other means, now known or hereafter invented, including xerography, photocopying and recording, or in any information or retrieval system, is forbidden without the prior written permission of both the publisher and copyright owner of this book.

Card Art Designs and Chart Art Designs by Melissa Alvarez
Card Meanings created by Melissa Alvarez
Published by arrangement with the author.

First Trade Paperback Printing: July 2010
10 9 8 7 6 5 4 3 2 1

> If you purchased this book without a cover, you should be aware that this book is stolen property. It was reposted as "unsold and destroyed" to the publisher, and neither the author nor the publisher has received any payment for this "stripped book."

To my readers,

    Chakra Divination is an ancient method of intuitive evaluation, which is used to energize, balance and cleanse the seven major chakras. Even though it's an ancient technique, it's also new, unique and non-traditional when compared to conventional methods of chakra work. This method was given to me from the higher realms as a way to examine the chakras through the use of intuition to uncover problems, find a course of action and to obtain ultimate balance within each chakra. This benefits you on a spiritual level. The artwork and card meanings were also divinely guided.

    Chakra Divination is a system you can use when your normal functioning energy flow feels disturbed. Through the use of the Chakra Divination charts, spreads and cards you can understand how to focus on the chakras using your intuition and perform intuitive chakra reading for yourself and others.

    I created the Chakra Divination Ultimate Balance Journal so you could record your readings and, after time passed while you worked on your course of action, you could add to the entry to note your accomplishments in attaining the solutions predicted in your reading for chakra balance. You can log one hundred Chakra Divination readings in this journal. Use it every time you conduct a reading.

    I hope you enjoy the Chakra Divination method of conducting energy readings with cards and charts to bring balance to your chakras. I'd love to hear from you. Visit me online!

Smiles,

Melissa Alvarez

ALSO BY MELISSA ALVAREZ

365 WAYS TO INCREASE YOUR FREQUENCY
(Llewellyn Publications – Available Fall 2011)
YOU'RE NOT CRAZY, YOU'RE CLAIRVOYANT
(Available Summer 2011)
THE ESSENTIAL GUIDE TO CHAKRA DIVINATION
CHAKRA DIVINATION CARDS & CHARTS ACTIVITY BOOK
CHAKRA DIVINATION CARDS
THE PHOENIX'S GUIDE TO SELF RENEWAL
YOUR COLOR POWER
ANALYZE YOUR HANDWRITING

BY MELISSA ALVAREZ
writing as ARIANA DUPRÉ

TALGORIAN PROPHECY
BENEATH A CHRISTMAS MOON (Anthology)
NIGHT VISIONS
BRIAR MOUNTAIN

All of the above are available at or can be ordered through your local bookstore or online at www.Llewellyn.com, www.CerridwenPress.com, www.Amazon.com, www.BN.com and other online retailers. Adrema Press books are also available at www.MelissaA.com and www.APsychicHaven.com.

Chakra Divination Ultimate Balance Journal

Today's Date: _____ **Time**: _____
Location: _____
Spread Chosen: _____
Chakra Cards: _____
_____

Problem Cards: _____
_____

Course of Action Cards: _____
_____

Solution Cards: _____
_____

My Initial Thoughts & Plan of Action: _____

Looking Back, Reflections on the Reading: _____

_____
_____
_____
_____
_____
_____
_____
_____
_____
_____
_____
_____
_____
_____
_____

Occurrences, Accomplishments & Results: _____

_____
_____
_____
_____
_____
_____
_____
_____
_____
_____
_____
_____
_____
_____
_____
_____
_____
_____
_____
_____
_____

Today's Date: _____ *Time*: _____
Location: _____
Spread Chosen: _____
Chakra Cards: _____
_____

Problem Cards:_____
_____

Course of Action Cards:_____
_____

Solution Cards:_____
_____

My Initial Thoughts & Plan of Action: _____
_____
_____
_____
_____
_____
_____
_____
_____
_____
_____
_____
_____
_____
_____
_____
_____
_____
_____
_____
_____
_____
_____
_____
_____
_____
_____

Looking Back, Reflections on the Reading: _____

_____
_____
_____
_____
_____
_____
_____
_____
_____
_____
_____
_____
_____
_____
_____
_____
_____

Occurrences, Accomplishments & Results: _____

_____
_____
_____
_____
_____
_____
_____
_____
_____
_____
_____
_____
_____
_____
_____
_____
_____
_____
_____
_____
_____

Chakra Divination Ultimate Balance Journal

Today's Date: _____ **Time**: _____
Location: _____
Spread Chosen: _____
Chakra Cards: _____
_____

Problem Cards:_____
_____

Course of Action Cards:_____
_____

Solution Cards:_____
_____

My Initial Thoughts & Plan of Action: _____
_____
_____
_____
_____
_____
_____
_____
_____
_____
_____
_____
_____
_____
_____
_____
_____
_____
_____
_____
_____
_____
_____
_____
_____

Chakra Divination Ultimate Balance Journal

Looking Back, Reflections on the Reading: _____

_____

Occurrences, Accomplishments & Results: _____

_____

Chakra Divination Ultimate Balance Journal

Today's Date: _____ **Time**: _____
Location: _____
Spread Chosen: _____
Chakra Cards: _____
_____

Problem Cards:_____
_____

Course of Action Cards:_____
_____

Solution Cards:_____
_____

My Initial Thoughts & Plan of Action: _____
_____
_____
_____
_____
_____
_____
_____
_____
_____
_____
_____
_____
_____
_____
_____
_____
_____
_____
_____
_____
_____
_____
_____
_____
_____

Looking Back, Reflections on the Reading: _____

_____
_____
_____
_____
_____
_____
_____
_____
_____
_____
_____
_____
_____
_____
_____
_____
_____
_____

Occurrences, Accomplishments & Results: _____

_____
_____
_____
_____
_____
_____
_____
_____
_____
_____
_____
_____
_____
_____
_____
_____
_____
_____
_____
_____

Chakra Divination Ultimate Balance Journal

Today's Date: _____ **Time**: _____
Location: _____
Spread Chosen: _____
Chakra Cards: _____

Problem Cards:_____

Course of Action Cards:_____

Solution Cards:_____

My Initial Thoughts & Plan of Action: _____
_____
_____
_____
_____
_____
_____
_____
_____
_____
_____
_____
_____
_____
_____
_____
_____
_____
_____
_____
_____
_____
_____
_____
_____

Looking Back, Reflections on the Reading: _____

Occurrences, Accomplishments & Results: _____

Today's Date: _____ ***Time***: _____
Location: _____
Spread Chosen: _____
Chakra Cards: _____
_____
Problem Cards: _____
_____
Course of Action Cards: _____
_____
Solution Cards: _____
_____

My Initial Thoughts & Plan of Action: _____
_____
_____
_____
_____
_____
_____
_____
_____
_____
_____
_____
_____
_____
_____
_____
_____
_____
_____
_____
_____
_____
_____
_____
_____
_____

Chakra Divination Ultimate Balance Journal

Looking Back, Reflections on the Reading: _____

_____
_____
_____
_____
_____
_____
_____
_____
_____
_____
_____
_____
_____
_____
_____
_____

Occurrences, Accomplishments & Results: _____

_____
_____
_____
_____
_____
_____
_____
_____
_____
_____
_____
_____
_____
_____
_____
_____
_____
_____
_____

Chakra Divination Ultimate Balance Journal

Today's Date: _____ **Time**: _____
Location: _____
Spread Chosen: _____
Chakra Cards: _____
_____

Problem Cards: _____
_____

Course of Action Cards: _____
_____

Solution Cards: _____
_____

My Initial Thoughts & Plan of Action: _____

Looking Back, Reflections on the Reading: _____

_____
_____
_____
_____
_____
_____
_____
_____
_____
_____
_____
_____
_____
_____
_____
_____

Occurrences, Accomplishments & Results: _____

_____
_____
_____
_____
_____
_____
_____
_____
_____
_____
_____
_____
_____
_____
_____
_____
_____
_____
_____
_____

Today's Date: _____ **Time**: _____
Location: _____
Spread Chosen: _____
Chakra Cards: _____

Problem Cards: _____

Course of Action Cards: _____

Solution Cards: _____

My Initial Thoughts & Plan of Action: _____
_____
_____
_____
_____
_____
_____
_____
_____
_____
_____
_____
_____
_____
_____
_____
_____
_____
_____
_____
_____
_____
_____
_____
_____
_____
_____
_____
_____

Looking Back, Reflections on the Reading: _____

_____
_____
_____
_____
_____
_____
_____
_____
_____
_____
_____
_____
_____
_____
_____
_____

Occurrences, Accomplishments & Results: _____

_____
_____
_____
_____
_____
_____
_____
_____
_____
_____
_____
_____
_____
_____
_____
_____
_____
_____
_____
_____

Today's Date: _____ **Time**: _____
Location: _____
Spread Chosen: _____
Chakra Cards: _____

Problem Cards:_____

Course of Action Cards:_____

Solution Cards:_____

My Initial Thoughts & Plan of Action: _____
_____
_____
_____
_____
_____
_____
_____
_____
_____
_____
_____
_____
_____
_____
_____
_____
_____
_____
_____
_____
_____
_____
_____
_____
_____
_____

Looking Back, Reflections on the Reading: _____

Occurrences, Accomplishments & Results: _____

Chakra Divination Ultimate Balance Journal

Today's Date: _____ **Time**: _____
Location: _____
Spread Chosen: _____
Chakra Cards: _____
_____

Problem Cards: _____
_____

Course of Action Cards: _____
_____

Solution Cards: _____
_____

My Initial Thoughts & Plan of Action: _____
_____
_____
_____
_____
_____
_____
_____
_____
_____
_____
_____
_____
_____
_____
_____
_____
_____
_____
_____
_____
_____
_____
_____
_____

Looking Back, Reflections on the Reading: _____

_____
_____
_____
_____
_____
_____
_____
_____
_____
_____
_____
_____
_____
_____
_____
_____
_____

Occurrences, Accomplishments & Results: _____

_____
_____
_____
_____
_____
_____
_____
_____
_____
_____
_____
_____
_____
_____
_____
_____
_____
_____
_____

Today's Date: _____ *Time*: _____
Location: _____
Spread Chosen: _____
Chakra Cards: _____
_____

Problem Cards: _____
_____

Course of Action Cards: _____
_____

Solution Cards: _____
_____

My Initial Thoughts & Plan of Action: _____
_____
_____
_____
_____
_____
_____
_____
_____
_____
_____
_____
_____
_____
_____
_____
_____
_____
_____
_____
_____
_____
_____
_____
_____
_____
_____
_____

Looking Back, Reflections on the Reading: _____

Occurrences, Accomplishments & Results: _____

Today's Date: _____ **Time**: _____
Location: _____
Spread Chosen: _____
Chakra Cards: _____

Problem Cards: _____

Course of Action Cards: _____

Solution Cards: _____

My Initial Thoughts & Plan of Action: _____
_____
_____
_____
_____
_____
_____
_____
_____
_____
_____
_____
_____
_____
_____
_____
_____
_____
_____
_____
_____
_____
_____
_____
_____
_____
_____
_____
_____

Looking Back, Reflections on the Reading: _____

_____
_____
_____
_____
_____
_____
_____
_____
_____
_____
_____
_____
_____
_____
_____
_____
_____

Occurrences, Accomplishments & Results: _____

_____
_____
_____
_____
_____
_____
_____
_____
_____
_____
_____
_____
_____
_____
_____
_____
_____
_____
_____
_____

Today's Date: _____ **Time**: _____
Location: _____
Spread Chosen: _____
Chakra Cards: _____
_____

Problem Cards: _____
_____

Course of Action Cards: _____
_____

Solution Cards: _____
_____

My Initial Thoughts & Plan of Action: _____
_____
_____
_____
_____
_____
_____
_____
_____
_____
_____
_____
_____
_____
_____
_____
_____
_____
_____
_____
_____
_____
_____
_____
_____
_____
_____

Looking Back, Reflections on the Reading: _____

_____
_____
_____
_____
_____
_____
_____
_____
_____
_____
_____
_____
_____
_____
_____

Occurrences, Accomplishments & Results: _____

_____
_____
_____
_____
_____
_____
_____
_____
_____
_____
_____
_____
_____
_____
_____
_____
_____
_____
_____

Today's Date: _____ *Time*: _____
Location: _____
Spread Chosen: _____
Chakra Cards: _____

Problem Cards: _____

Course of Action Cards: _____

Solution Cards: _____

My Initial Thoughts & Plan of Action: _____
_____
_____
_____
_____
_____
_____
_____
_____
_____
_____
_____
_____
_____
_____
_____
_____
_____
_____
_____
_____
_____
_____
_____
_____
_____
_____
_____
_____
_____

Looking Back, Reflections on the Reading: _____

Occurrences, Accomplishments & Results: _____

Today's Date: _____ ***Time***: _____
Location: _____
Spread Chosen: _____
Chakra Cards: _____
_____

Problem Cards:_____
_____

Course of Action Cards:_____
_____

Solution Cards:_____
_____

My Initial Thoughts & Plan of Action: _____
_____
_____
_____
_____
_____
_____
_____
_____
_____
_____
_____
_____
_____
_____
_____
_____
_____
_____
_____
_____
_____
_____
_____
_____
_____
_____

Looking Back, Reflections on the Reading: _____

Occurrences, Accomplishments & Results: _____

Today's Date: _____ **Time**: _____

Location: _____

Spread Chosen: _____

Chakra Cards: _____

_____

Problem Cards: _____

_____

Course of Action Cards: _____

_____

Solution Cards: _____

_____

My Initial Thoughts & Plan of Action: _____

_____
_____
_____
_____
_____
_____
_____
_____
_____
_____
_____
_____
_____
_____
_____
_____
_____
_____
_____
_____
_____
_____
_____
_____
_____
_____

Looking Back, Reflections on the Reading: _____

_____
_____
_____
_____
_____
_____
_____
_____
_____
_____
_____
_____
_____
_____
_____
_____
_____

Occurrences, Accomplishments & Results: _____

_____
_____
_____
_____
_____
_____
_____
_____
_____
_____
_____
_____
_____
_____
_____
_____
_____
_____
_____
_____
_____

Today's Date: _____ ***Time***: _____
Location: _____
Spread Chosen: _____
Chakra Cards: _____

Problem Cards: _____

Course of Action Cards: _____

Solution Cards: _____

My Initial Thoughts & Plan of Action: _____
_____
_____
_____
_____
_____
_____
_____
_____
_____
_____
_____
_____
_____
_____
_____
_____
_____
_____
_____
_____
_____
_____
_____
_____
_____
_____

Looking Back, Reflections on the Reading: _____

_____
_____
_____
_____
_____
_____
_____
_____
_____
_____
_____
_____
_____
_____
_____
_____

Occurrences, Accomplishments & Results: _____

_____
_____
_____
_____
_____
_____
_____
_____
_____
_____
_____
_____
_____
_____
_____
_____
_____
_____

Chakra Divination Ultimate Balance Journal

Today's Date: _____ **Time**: _____
Location: _____
Spread Chosen: _____
Chakra Cards: _____

Problem Cards:_____

Course of Action Cards:_____

Solution Cards:_____

My Initial Thoughts & Plan of Action: _____
_____
_____
_____
_____
_____
_____
_____
_____
_____
_____
_____
_____
_____
_____
_____
_____
_____
_____
_____
_____
_____
_____
_____
_____
_____

Chakra Divination Ultimate Balance Journal

Looking Back, Reflections on the Reading: _____

_____
_____
_____
_____
_____
_____
_____
_____
_____
_____
_____
_____
_____
_____
_____
_____
_____

Occurrences, Accomplishments & Results: _____

_____
_____
_____
_____
_____
_____
_____
_____
_____
_____
_____
_____
_____
_____
_____
_____
_____
_____
_____
_____

Chakra Divination Ultimate Balance Journal

Today's Date: _____ **Time**: _____
Location: _____
Spread Chosen: _____
Chakra Cards: _____

Problem Cards: _____

Course of Action Cards: _____

Solution Cards: _____

My Initial Thoughts & Plan of Action: _____
_____
_____
_____
_____
_____
_____
_____
_____
_____
_____
_____
_____
_____
_____
_____
_____
_____
_____
_____
_____
_____
_____
_____
_____
_____
_____

Looking Back, Reflections on the Reading: _____

_____
_____
_____
_____
_____
_____
_____
_____
_____
_____
_____
_____
_____
_____
_____

Occurrences, Accomplishments & Results: _____

_____
_____
_____
_____
_____
_____
_____
_____
_____
_____
_____
_____
_____
_____
_____
_____
_____
_____
_____

Chakra Divination Ultimate Balance Journal

Today's Date: _____ ***Time***: _____
Location: _____
Spread Chosen: _____
Chakra Cards: _____
_____

Problem Cards:_____
_____

Course of Action Cards:_____
_____

Solution Cards:_____
_____

My Initial Thoughts & Plan of Action: _____
_____
_____
_____
_____
_____
_____
_____
_____
_____
_____
_____
_____
_____
_____
_____
_____
_____
_____
_____
_____
_____
_____
_____
_____
_____

Looking Back, Reflections on the Reading: _____

_____
_____
_____
_____
_____
_____
_____
_____
_____
_____
_____
_____
_____
_____
_____
_____

Occurrences, Accomplishments & Results: _____

_____
_____
_____
_____
_____
_____
_____
_____
_____
_____
_____
_____
_____
_____
_____
_____
_____
_____
_____
_____

Chakra Divination Ultimate Balance Journal

Today's Date: _____ ***Time***: _____
Location: _____
Spread Chosen: _____
Chakra Cards: _____
_____

Problem Cards:_____
_____

Course of Action Cards:_____
_____

Solution Cards:_____
_____

My Initial Thoughts & Plan of Action: _____
_____
_____
_____
_____
_____
_____
_____
_____
_____
_____
_____
_____
_____
_____
_____
_____
_____
_____
_____
_____
_____
_____

Looking Back, Reflections on the Reading: _____

_____
_____
_____
_____
_____
_____
_____
_____
_____
_____
_____
_____
_____
_____
_____

Occurrences, Accomplishments & Results: _____

_____
_____
_____
_____
_____
_____
_____
_____
_____
_____
_____
_____
_____
_____
_____
_____
_____
_____
_____
_____

Chakra Divination Ultimate Balance Journal

Today's Date: _____ **Time**: _____
Location: _____
Spread Chosen: _____
Chakra Cards: _____
_____

Problem Cards: _____
_____

Course of Action Cards: _____
_____

Solution Cards: _____
_____

My Initial Thoughts & Plan of Action: _____
_____
_____
_____
_____
_____
_____
_____
_____
_____
_____
_____
_____
_____
_____
_____
_____
_____
_____
_____
_____
_____
_____
_____
_____
_____

Looking Back, Reflections on the Reading: _____

_____
_____
_____
_____
_____
_____
_____
_____
_____
_____
_____
_____
_____
_____
_____

Occurrences, Accomplishments & Results: _____

_____
_____
_____
_____
_____
_____
_____
_____
_____
_____
_____
_____
_____
_____
_____
_____
_____
_____
_____

Today's Date: _____ ***Time***: _____
Location: _____
Spread Chosen: _____
Chakra Cards: _____
_____

Problem Cards: _____
_____

Course of Action Cards: _____
_____

Solution Cards: _____
_____

My Initial Thoughts & Plan of Action: _____
_____
_____
_____
_____
_____
_____
_____
_____
_____
_____
_____
_____
_____
_____
_____
_____
_____
_____
_____
_____
_____
_____
_____
_____
_____
_____

Looking Back, Reflections on the Reading: _____

Occurrences, Accomplishments & Results: _____

Today's Date: _____ ***Time***: _____
Location: _____
Spread Chosen: _____
Chakra Cards: _____

Problem Cards: _____

Course of Action Cards: _____

Solution Cards: _____

My Initial Thoughts & Plan of Action: _____
_____
_____
_____
_____
_____
_____
_____
_____
_____
_____
_____
_____
_____
_____
_____
_____
_____
_____
_____
_____
_____
_____
_____
_____

Looking Back, Reflections on the Reading: _____

_____
_____
_____
_____
_____
_____
_____
_____
_____
_____
_____
_____
_____
_____
_____

Occurrences, Accomplishments & Results: _____

_____
_____
_____
_____
_____
_____
_____
_____
_____
_____
_____
_____
_____
_____
_____
_____
_____
_____
_____

Today's Date: _____ **Time**: _____
Location: _____
Spread Chosen: _____
Chakra Cards: _____
_____

Problem Cards: _____
_____

Course of Action Cards: _____
_____

Solution Cards: _____
_____

My Initial Thoughts & Plan of Action: _____
_____
_____
_____
_____
_____
_____
_____
_____
_____
_____
_____
_____
_____
_____
_____
_____
_____
_____
_____
_____
_____
_____
_____
_____
_____
_____
_____

Looking Back, Reflections on the Reading: _____

_____
_____
_____
_____
_____
_____
_____
_____
_____
_____
_____
_____
_____
_____
_____
_____
_____

Occurrences, Accomplishments & Results: _____

_____
_____
_____
_____
_____
_____
_____
_____
_____
_____
_____
_____
_____
_____
_____
_____
_____
_____
_____
_____
_____

Today's Date: _____ ***Time***: _____
Location: _____
Spread Chosen: _____
Chakra Cards: _____

Problem Cards: _____

Course of Action Cards: _____

Solution Cards: _____

My Initial Thoughts & Plan of Action: _____
_____
_____
_____
_____
_____
_____
_____
_____
_____
_____
_____
_____
_____
_____
_____
_____
_____
_____
_____
_____
_____
_____
_____
_____
_____
_____

Looking Back, Reflections on the Reading: _____

Occurrences, Accomplishments & Results: _____

Today's Date: _____ **Time**: _____

Location: _____

Spread Chosen: _____

Chakra Cards: _____
_____

Problem Cards:_____
_____

Course of Action Cards:_____
_____

Solution Cards:_____
_____

My Initial Thoughts & Plan of Action: _____
_____
_____
_____
_____
_____
_____
_____
_____
_____
_____
_____
_____
_____
_____
_____
_____
_____
_____
_____
_____
_____
_____
_____
_____
_____

Looking Back, Reflections on the Reading: _____

Occurrences, Accomplishments & Results: _____

Today's Date: _____ **Time**: _____
Location: _____
Spread Chosen: _____
Chakra Cards: _____
_____

Problem Cards:_____
_____

Course of Action Cards:_____
_____

Solution Cards:_____
_____

My Initial Thoughts & Plan of Action: _____
_____
_____
_____
_____
_____
_____
_____
_____
_____
_____
_____
_____
_____
_____
_____
_____
_____
_____
_____
_____
_____
_____
_____
_____
_____

Looking Back, Reflections on the Reading: _____

Occurrences, Accomplishments & Results: _____

Today's Date: _____ *Time*: _____
Location: _____
Spread Chosen: _____
Chakra Cards: _____

Problem Cards: _____

Course of Action Cards: _____

Solution Cards: _____

My Initial Thoughts & Plan of Action: _____

_____
_____
_____
_____
_____
_____
_____
_____
_____
_____
_____
_____
_____
_____
_____
_____
_____
_____
_____
_____
_____
_____
_____
_____
_____

Looking Back, Reflections on the Reading: _____

Occurrences, Accomplishments & Results: _____

Today's Date: _____ ***Time***: _____
Location: _____
Spread Chosen: _____
Chakra Cards: _____

Problem Cards:_____

Course of Action Cards:_____

Solution Cards:_____

My Initial Thoughts & Plan of Action: _____
_____
_____
_____
_____
_____
_____
_____
_____
_____
_____
_____
_____
_____
_____
_____
_____
_____
_____
_____
_____
_____
_____
_____
_____

Looking Back, Reflections on the Reading: _____

Occurrences, Accomplishments & Results: _____

Chakra Divination Ultimate Balance Journal

Today's Date: _____ **Time**: _____
Location: _____
Spread Chosen: _____
Chakra Cards: _____
_____

Problem Cards:_____
_____

Course of Action Cards:_____
_____

Solution Cards:_____
_____

My Initial Thoughts & Plan of Action: _____
_____
_____
_____
_____
_____
_____
_____
_____
_____
_____
_____
_____
_____
_____
_____
_____
_____
_____
_____
_____
_____
_____
_____
_____
_____
_____
_____
_____

Looking Back, Reflections on the Reading: _____

_____
_____
_____
_____
_____
_____
_____
_____
_____
_____
_____
_____
_____
_____
_____
_____
_____

Occurrences, Accomplishments & Results: _____

_____
_____
_____
_____
_____
_____
_____
_____
_____
_____
_____
_____
_____
_____
_____
_____
_____
_____
_____
_____

Chakra Divination Ultimate Balance Journal

Today's Date: _____ ***Time***: _____
Location: _____
Spread Chosen: _____
Chakra Cards: _____

Problem Cards: _____

Course of Action Cards: _____

Solution Cards: _____

My Initial Thoughts & Plan of Action: _____

_____
_____
_____
_____
_____
_____
_____
_____
_____
_____
_____
_____
_____
_____
_____
_____
_____
_____
_____
_____
_____
_____
_____
_____
_____

Looking Back, Reflections on the Reading: _____

Occurrences, Accomplishments & Results: _____

Today's Date: _____ **Time**: _____
Location: _____
Spread Chosen: _____
Chakra Cards: _____
_____

Problem Cards:_____
_____

Course of Action Cards:_____
_____

Solution Cards:_____
_____

My Initial Thoughts & Plan of Action: _____
_____
_____
_____
_____
_____
_____
_____
_____
_____
_____
_____
_____
_____
_____
_____
_____
_____
_____
_____
_____
_____
_____
_____
_____
_____
_____

Looking Back, Reflections on the Reading: _____

_____
_____
_____
_____
_____
_____
_____
_____
_____
_____
_____
_____
_____
_____
_____

Occurrences, Accomplishments & Results: _____

_____
_____
_____
_____
_____
_____
_____
_____
_____
_____
_____
_____
_____
_____
_____
_____
_____
_____
_____
_____

Chakra Divination Ultimate Balance Journal

Today's Date: _____ **Time**: _____
Location: _____
Spread Chosen: _____
Chakra Cards: _____

Problem Cards: _____

Course of Action Cards: _____

Solution Cards: _____

My Initial Thoughts & Plan of Action: _____
_____
_____
_____
_____
_____
_____
_____
_____
_____
_____
_____
_____
_____
_____
_____
_____
_____
_____
_____
_____
_____
_____
_____
_____
_____
_____

Looking Back, Reflections on the Reading: _____

_____
_____
_____
_____
_____
_____
_____
_____
_____
_____
_____
_____
_____
_____
_____

Occurrences, Accomplishments & Results: _____

_____
_____
_____
_____
_____
_____
_____
_____
_____
_____
_____
_____
_____
_____
_____
_____
_____
_____
_____
_____

Chakra Divination Ultimate Balance Journal

Today's Date: _____ ***Time***: _____
Location: _____
Spread Chosen: _____
Chakra Cards: _____

Problem Cards: _____

Course of Action Cards: _____

Solution Cards: _____

My Initial Thoughts & Plan of Action: _____
_____
_____
_____
_____
_____
_____
_____
_____
_____
_____
_____
_____
_____
_____
_____
_____
_____
_____
_____
_____
_____
_____
_____
_____
_____
_____
_____
_____

Looking Back, Reflections on the Reading: _____

_____
_____
_____
_____
_____
_____
_____
_____
_____
_____
_____
_____
_____
_____
_____
_____
_____

Occurrences, Accomplishments & Results: _____

_____
_____
_____
_____
_____
_____
_____
_____
_____
_____
_____
_____
_____
_____
_____
_____
_____
_____
_____
_____

Chakra Divination Ultimate Balance Journal

Today's Date: _____ **Time**: _____
Location: _____
Spread Chosen: _____
Chakra Cards: _____
_____

Problem Cards:_____
_____

Course of Action Cards:_____
_____

Solution Cards:_____
_____

My Initial Thoughts & Plan of Action: _____
_____
_____
_____
_____
_____
_____
_____
_____
_____
_____
_____
_____
_____
_____
_____
_____
_____
_____
_____
_____
_____
_____
_____
_____
_____
_____

Looking Back, Reflections on the Reading: _____

Occurrences, Accomplishments & Results: _____

Chakra Divination Ultimate Balance Journal

Today's Date: _____ **Time**: _____
Location: _____
Spread Chosen: _____
Chakra Cards: _____

Problem Cards:_____

Course of Action Cards:_____

Solution Cards:_____

My Initial Thoughts & Plan of Action: _____
_____
_____
_____
_____
_____
_____
_____
_____
_____
_____
_____
_____
_____
_____
_____
_____
_____
_____
_____
_____
_____
_____
_____
_____
_____

Looking Back, Reflections on the Reading: _____

_____
_____
_____
_____
_____
_____
_____
_____
_____
_____
_____
_____
_____
_____
_____
_____

Occurrences, Accomplishments & Results: _____

_____
_____
_____
_____
_____
_____
_____
_____
_____
_____
_____
_____
_____
_____
_____
_____
_____
_____
_____
_____

Chakra Divination Ultimate Balance Journal

Today's Date: _____ ***Time***: _____
Location: _____
Spread Chosen: _____
Chakra Cards: _____
_____

Problem Cards: _____
_____

Course of Action Cards: _____
_____

Solution Cards: _____
_____

My Initial Thoughts & Plan of Action: _____
_____
_____
_____
_____
_____
_____
_____
_____
_____
_____
_____
_____
_____
_____
_____
_____
_____
_____
_____
_____
_____
_____
_____
_____
_____

Looking Back, Reflections on the Reading: _____

_____
_____
_____
_____
_____
_____
_____
_____
_____
_____
_____
_____
_____
_____
_____
_____
_____

Occurrences, Accomplishments & Results: _____

_____
_____
_____
_____
_____
_____
_____
_____
_____
_____
_____
_____
_____
_____
_____
_____
_____
_____
_____
_____

Chakra Divination Ultimate Balance Journal

Today's Date: _____ **Time**: _____
Location: _____
Spread Chosen: _____
Chakra Cards: _____

Problem Cards: _____

Course of Action Cards: _____

Solution Cards: _____

My Initial Thoughts & Plan of Action: _____
_____
_____
_____
_____
_____
_____
_____
_____
_____
_____
_____
_____
_____
_____
_____
_____
_____
_____
_____
_____
_____
_____
_____

Looking Back, Reflections on the Reading: _____

Occurrences, Accomplishments & Results: _____

Chakra Divination Ultimate Balance Journal

Today's Date: _____ **Time**: _____

Location: _____

Spread Chosen: _____

Chakra Cards: _____

Problem Cards:_____

Course of Action Cards:_____

Solution Cards:_____

My Initial Thoughts & Plan of Action: _____

_____
_____
_____
_____
_____
_____
_____
_____
_____
_____
_____
_____
_____
_____
_____
_____
_____
_____
_____
_____
_____
_____
_____
_____
_____

Looking Back, Reflections on the Reading: _____

Occurrences, Accomplishments & Results: _____

Today's Date: _____ **Time**: _____
Location: _____
Spread Chosen: _____
Chakra Cards: _____
_____

Problem Cards: _____
_____

Course of Action Cards: _____
_____

Solution Cards: _____
_____

My Initial Thoughts & Plan of Action: _____
_____

Looking Back, Reflections on the Reading: _____

Occurrences, Accomplishments & Results: _____

Chakra Divination Ultimate Balance Journal

Today's Date: _____ **Time**: _____

Location: _____

Spread Chosen: _____

Chakra Cards: _____
_____

Problem Cards: _____
_____

Course of Action Cards: _____
_____

Solution Cards: _____
_____

My Initial Thoughts & Plan of Action: _____
_____
_____
_____
_____
_____
_____
_____
_____
_____
_____
_____
_____
_____
_____
_____
_____
_____
_____
_____
_____
_____
_____
_____
_____
_____

Looking Back, Reflections on the Reading: _____

Occurrences, Accomplishments & Results: _____

Chakra Divination Ultimate Balance Journal

Today's Date: _____ **Time**: _____
Location: _____
Spread Chosen: _____
Chakra Cards: _____

Problem Cards:_____

Course of Action Cards:_____

Solution Cards:_____

My Initial Thoughts & Plan of Action: _____
_____
_____
_____
_____
_____
_____
_____
_____
_____
_____
_____
_____
_____
_____
_____
_____
_____
_____
_____
_____
_____
_____
_____

Looking Back, Reflections on the Reading: _____

Occurrences, Accomplishments & Results: _____

Today's Date: _____ *Time*: _____
Location: _____
Spread Chosen: _____
Chakra Cards: _____
_____

Problem Cards:_____
_____

Course of Action Cards:_____
_____

Solution Cards:_____
_____

My Initial Thoughts & Plan of Action: _____
_____
_____
_____
_____
_____
_____
_____
_____
_____
_____
_____
_____
_____
_____
_____
_____
_____
_____
_____
_____
_____
_____
_____
_____
_____
_____

Looking Back, Reflections on the Reading: _____

_____
_____
_____
_____
_____
_____
_____
_____
_____
_____
_____
_____
_____
_____
_____
_____
_____
_____

Occurrences, Accomplishments & Results: _____

_____
_____
_____
_____
_____
_____
_____
_____
_____
_____
_____
_____
_____
_____
_____
_____
_____
_____
_____
_____
_____

Chakra Divination Ultimate Balance Journal

Today's Date: _____ ***Time***: _____
Location: _____
Spread Chosen: _____
Chakra Cards: _____

Problem Cards: _____

Course of Action Cards: _____

Solution Cards: _____

My Initial Thoughts & Plan of Action: _____
_____
_____
_____
_____
_____
_____
_____
_____
_____
_____
_____
_____
_____
_____
_____
_____
_____
_____
_____
_____
_____
_____
_____
_____
_____
_____
_____

Looking Back, Reflections on the Reading: _____

Occurrences, Accomplishments & Results: _____

Today's Date: _____ *Time*: _____
Location: _____
Spread Chosen: _____
Chakra Cards: _____
_____

Problem Cards: _____
_____

Course of Action Cards: _____
_____

Solution Cards: _____
_____

My Initial Thoughts & Plan of Action: _____
_____
_____
_____
_____
_____
_____
_____
_____
_____
_____
_____
_____
_____
_____
_____
_____
_____
_____
_____
_____
_____
_____
_____
_____
_____
_____

Looking Back, Reflections on the Reading: _____

_____
_____
_____
_____
_____
_____
_____
_____
_____
_____
_____
_____
_____
_____
_____
_____
_____

Occurrences, Accomplishments & Results: _____

_____
_____
_____
_____
_____
_____
_____
_____
_____
_____
_____
_____
_____
_____
_____
_____
_____
_____
_____
_____

Chakra Divination Ultimate Balance Journal

Today's Date: _____ **Time**: _____
Location: _____
Spread Chosen: _____
Chakra Cards: _____

Problem Cards: _____

Course of Action Cards: _____

Solution Cards: _____

My Initial Thoughts & Plan of Action: _____

_____
_____
_____
_____
_____
_____
_____
_____
_____
_____
_____
_____
_____
_____
_____
_____
_____
_____
_____
_____
_____
_____
_____
_____
_____
_____

Looking Back, Reflections on the Reading: _____

_____
_____
_____
_____
_____
_____
_____
_____
_____
_____
_____
_____
_____
_____
_____
_____

Occurrences, Accomplishments & Results: _____

_____
_____
_____
_____
_____
_____
_____
_____
_____
_____
_____
_____
_____
_____
_____
_____
_____
_____
_____
_____
_____

Today's Date: _____ **Time**: _____
Location: _____
Spread Chosen: _____
Chakra Cards: _____
_____

Problem Cards:_____
_____

Course of Action Cards:_____
_____

Solution Cards:_____
_____

My Initial Thoughts & Plan of Action: _____
_____
_____
_____
_____
_____
_____
_____
_____
_____
_____
_____
_____
_____
_____
_____
_____
_____
_____
_____
_____
_____
_____
_____

Looking Back, Reflections on the Reading: _____

Occurrences, Accomplishments & Results: _____

Today's Date: _____ **Time**: _____
Location: _____
Spread Chosen: _____
Chakra Cards: _____
_____

Problem Cards: _____
_____

Course of Action Cards: _____
_____

Solution Cards: _____
_____

My Initial Thoughts & Plan of Action: _____
_____
_____
_____
_____
_____
_____
_____
_____
_____
_____
_____
_____
_____
_____
_____
_____
_____
_____
_____
_____
_____
_____
_____
_____

Looking Back, Reflections on the Reading: _____

_____
_____
_____
_____
_____
_____
_____
_____
_____
_____
_____
_____
_____
_____
_____

Occurrences, Accomplishments & Results: _____

_____
_____
_____
_____
_____
_____
_____
_____
_____
_____
_____
_____
_____
_____
_____
_____
_____
_____
_____

Chakra Divination Ultimate Balance Journal

Today's Date: _____ *Time*: _____
Location: _____
Spread Chosen: _____
Chakra Cards: _____

Problem Cards:_____

Course of Action Cards:_____

Solution Cards:_____

My Initial Thoughts & Plan of Action: _____

Looking Back, Reflections on the Reading: _____

Occurrences, Accomplishments & Results: _____

Chakra Divination Ultimate Balance Journal

Today's Date: _____ **Time**: _____
Location: _____
Spread Chosen: _____
Chakra Cards: _____
_____

Problem Cards: _____
_____

Course of Action Cards: _____
_____

Solution Cards: _____
_____

My Initial Thoughts & Plan of Action: _____
_____
_____
_____
_____
_____
_____
_____
_____
_____
_____
_____
_____
_____
_____
_____
_____
_____
_____
_____
_____
_____
_____
_____
_____
_____

Looking Back, Reflections on the Reading: _____

_____
_____
_____
_____
_____
_____
_____
_____
_____
_____
_____
_____
_____
_____

Occurrences, Accomplishments & Results: _____

_____
_____
_____
_____
_____
_____
_____
_____
_____
_____
_____
_____
_____
_____
_____
_____
_____
_____

Today's Date: _____ *Time*: _____
Location: _____
Spread Chosen: _____
Chakra Cards: _____

Problem Cards: _____

Course of Action Cards: _____

Solution Cards: _____

My Initial Thoughts & Plan of Action: _____
_____
_____
_____
_____
_____
_____
_____
_____
_____
_____
_____
_____
_____
_____
_____
_____
_____
_____
_____
_____
_____
_____
_____
_____
_____

Looking Back, Reflections on the Reading: _____

_____
_____
_____
_____
_____
_____
_____
_____
_____
_____
_____
_____
_____
_____
_____

Occurrences, Accomplishments & Results: _____

_____
_____
_____
_____
_____
_____
_____
_____
_____
_____
_____
_____
_____
_____
_____
_____
_____
_____

Chakra Divination Ultimate Balance Journal

Today's Date: _____ **Time**: _____
Location: _____
Spread Chosen: _____
Chakra Cards: _____
_____

Problem Cards: _____
_____

Course of Action Cards: _____
_____

Solution Cards: _____
_____

My Initial Thoughts & Plan of Action: _____
_____
_____
_____
_____
_____
_____
_____
_____
_____
_____
_____
_____
_____
_____
_____
_____
_____
_____
_____
_____
_____
_____
_____
_____
_____
_____
_____

Looking Back, Reflections on the Reading: _____

_____
_____
_____
_____
_____
_____
_____
_____
_____
_____
_____
_____
_____
_____

Occurrences, Accomplishments & Results: _____

_____
_____
_____
_____
_____
_____
_____
_____
_____
_____
_____
_____
_____
_____
_____
_____
_____

Chakra Divination Ultimate Balance Journal

Today's Date: _____ ***Time***: _____
Location: _____
Spread Chosen: _____
Chakra Cards: _____

Problem Cards:_____

Course of Action Cards:_____

Solution Cards:_____

My Initial Thoughts & Plan of Action: _____
_____
_____
_____
_____
_____
_____
_____
_____
_____
_____
_____
_____
_____
_____
_____
_____
_____
_____
_____
_____
_____
_____
_____
_____
_____
_____

Looking Back, Reflections on the Reading: _____

_____
_____
_____
_____
_____
_____
_____
_____
_____
_____
_____
_____
_____
_____
_____
_____
_____
_____

Occurrences, Accomplishments & Results: _____

_____
_____
_____
_____
_____
_____
_____
_____
_____
_____
_____
_____
_____
_____
_____
_____
_____
_____
_____
_____
_____

Today's Date: _____ ***Time***: _____

Location: _____

Spread Chosen: _____

Chakra Cards: _____

Problem Cards: _____

Course of Action Cards: _____

Solution Cards: _____

My Initial Thoughts & Plan of Action: _____

_____
_____
_____
_____
_____
_____
_____
_____
_____
_____
_____
_____
_____
_____
_____
_____
_____
_____
_____
_____
_____
_____
_____
_____
_____

Looking Back, Reflections on the Reading: _____

Occurrences, Accomplishments & Results: _____

Chakra Divination Ultimate Balance Journal

Today's Date: _____ ***Time***: _____
Location: _____
Spread Chosen: _____
Chakra Cards: _____
_____

Problem Cards:_____
_____

Course of Action Cards:_____
_____

Solution Cards:_____
_____

My Initial Thoughts & Plan of Action: _____
_____
_____
_____
_____
_____
_____
_____
_____
_____
_____
_____
_____
_____
_____
_____
_____
_____
_____
_____
_____
_____
_____
_____
_____
_____

Looking Back, Reflections on the Reading: _____

Occurrences, Accomplishments & Results: _____

Chakra Divination Ultimate Balance Journal

Today's Date: _____ **Time**: _____
Location: _____
Spread Chosen: _____
Chakra Cards: _____

Problem Cards: _____

Course of Action Cards: _____

Solution Cards: _____

My Initial Thoughts & Plan of Action: _____
_____
_____
_____
_____
_____
_____
_____
_____
_____
_____
_____
_____
_____
_____
_____
_____
_____
_____
_____
_____
_____
_____
_____
_____

Looking Back, Reflections on the Reading: _____

_____
_____
_____
_____
_____
_____
_____
_____
_____
_____
_____
_____
_____
_____
_____
_____

Occurrences, Accomplishments & Results: _____

_____
_____
_____
_____
_____
_____
_____
_____
_____
_____
_____
_____
_____
_____
_____
_____
_____
_____
_____
_____
_____
_____

Today's Date: _____ **Time**: _____
Location: _____
Spread Chosen: _____
Chakra Cards: _____

Problem Cards: _____

Course of Action Cards: _____

Solution Cards: _____

My Initial Thoughts & Plan of Action: _____
_____
_____
_____
_____
_____
_____
_____
_____
_____
_____
_____
_____
_____
_____
_____
_____
_____
_____
_____
_____
_____
_____
_____

Looking Back, Reflections on the Reading: _____

_____
_____
_____
_____
_____
_____
_____
_____
_____
_____
_____
_____
_____
_____
_____

Occurrences, Accomplishments & Results: _____

_____
_____
_____
_____
_____
_____
_____
_____
_____
_____
_____
_____
_____
_____
_____
_____
_____
_____
_____

Chakra Divination Ultimate Balance Journal

Today's Date: _____ ***Time***: _____
Location: _____
Spread Chosen: _____
Chakra Cards: _____
_____

Problem Cards: _____
_____

Course of Action Cards: _____
_____

Solution Cards: _____
_____

My Initial Thoughts & Plan of Action: _____
_____
_____
_____
_____
_____
_____
_____
_____
_____
_____
_____
_____
_____
_____
_____
_____
_____
_____
_____
_____
_____
_____
_____
_____

Looking Back, Reflections on the Reading: _____

_____
_____
_____
_____
_____
_____
_____
_____
_____
_____
_____
_____
_____
_____
_____
_____
_____

Occurrences, Accomplishments & Results: _____

_____
_____
_____
_____
_____
_____
_____
_____
_____
_____
_____
_____
_____
_____
_____
_____
_____
_____
_____
_____

Chakra Divination Ultimate Balance Journal

Today's Date: _____ **Time**: _____
Location: _____
Spread Chosen: _____
Chakra Cards: _____
_____

Problem Cards: _____
_____

Course of Action Cards: _____
_____

Solution Cards: _____
_____

My Initial Thoughts & Plan of Action: _____
_____
_____
_____
_____
_____
_____
_____
_____
_____
_____
_____
_____
_____
_____
_____
_____
_____
_____
_____
_____
_____
_____

Looking Back, Reflections on the Reading: _____

Occurrences, Accomplishments & Results: _____

Chakra Divination Ultimate Balance Journal

Today's Date: _____ ***Time***: _____
Location: _____
Spread Chosen: _____
Chakra Cards: _____

Problem Cards: _____

Course of Action Cards: _____

Solution Cards: _____

My Initial Thoughts & Plan of Action: _____
_____
_____
_____
_____
_____
_____
_____
_____
_____
_____
_____
_____
_____
_____
_____
_____
_____
_____
_____
_____
_____
_____
_____
_____
_____

Looking Back, Reflections on the Reading: _____

_____
_____
_____
_____
_____
_____
_____
_____
_____
_____
_____
_____
_____
_____
_____
_____
_____

Occurrences, Accomplishments & Results: _____

_____
_____
_____
_____
_____
_____
_____
_____
_____
_____
_____
_____
_____
_____
_____
_____
_____
_____
_____

Chakra Divination Ultimate Balance Journal

Today's Date: _____ **Time**: _____
Location: _____
Spread Chosen: _____
Chakra Cards: _____
_____

Problem Cards:_____
_____

Course of Action Cards:_____
_____

Solution Cards:_____
_____

My Initial Thoughts & Plan of Action: _____
_____
_____
_____
_____
_____
_____
_____
_____
_____
_____
_____
_____
_____
_____
_____
_____
_____
_____
_____
_____
_____
_____
_____
_____
_____

Looking Back, Reflections on the Reading: _____

Occurrences, Accomplishments & Results: _____

Chakra Divination Ultimate Balance Journal

Today's Date: _____ **Time**: _____
Location: _____
Spread Chosen: _____
Chakra Cards: _____
_____

Problem Cards: _____
_____

Course of Action Cards: _____
_____

Solution Cards: _____
_____

My Initial Thoughts & Plan of Action: _____
_____
_____
_____
_____
_____
_____
_____
_____
_____
_____
_____
_____
_____
_____
_____
_____
_____
_____
_____
_____
_____
_____
_____

Looking Back, Reflections on the Reading: _____

_____
_____
_____
_____
_____
_____
_____
_____
_____
_____
_____
_____
_____
_____
_____

Occurrences, Accomplishments & Results: _____

_____
_____
_____
_____
_____
_____
_____
_____
_____
_____
_____
_____
_____
_____
_____
_____
_____
_____

Chakra Divination Ultimate Balance Journal

Today's Date: _____ **Time**: _____
Location: _____
Spread Chosen: _____
Chakra Cards: _____
_____

Problem Cards: _____
_____

Course of Action Cards: _____
_____

Solution Cards: _____
_____

My Initial Thoughts & Plan of Action: _____

Looking Back, Reflections on the Reading: _____

Occurrences, Accomplishments & Results: _____

Today's Date: _____ *Time*: _____
Location: _____
Spread Chosen: _____
Chakra Cards: _____

Problem Cards: _____

Course of Action Cards: _____

Solution Cards: _____

My Initial Thoughts & Plan of Action: _____
_____
_____
_____
_____
_____
_____
_____
_____
_____
_____
_____
_____
_____
_____
_____
_____
_____
_____
_____
_____
_____
_____
_____
_____
_____

Looking Back, Reflections on the Reading: _____

_____
_____
_____
_____
_____
_____
_____
_____
_____
_____
_____
_____
_____
_____
_____
_____

Occurrences, Accomplishments & Results: _____

_____
_____
_____
_____
_____
_____
_____
_____
_____
_____
_____
_____
_____
_____
_____
_____
_____
_____
_____

Chakra Divination Ultimate Balance Journal

Today's Date: _____ **Time**: _____
Location: _____
Spread Chosen: _____
Chakra Cards: _____

Problem Cards: _____

Course of Action Cards: _____

Solution Cards: _____

My Initial Thoughts & Plan of Action: _____
_____
_____
_____
_____
_____
_____
_____
_____
_____
_____
_____
_____
_____
_____
_____
_____
_____
_____
_____
_____
_____
_____
_____
_____
_____
_____

Looking Back, Reflections on the Reading: _____

Occurrences, Accomplishments & Results: _____

Today's Date: _____ **Time**: _____
Location: _____
Spread Chosen: _____
Chakra Cards: _____
_____

Problem Cards: _____
_____

Course of Action Cards: _____
_____

Solution Cards: _____
_____

My Initial Thoughts & Plan of Action: _____
_____
_____
_____
_____
_____
_____
_____
_____
_____
_____
_____
_____
_____
_____
_____
_____
_____
_____
_____
_____
_____
_____
_____
_____
_____

Looking Back, Reflections on the Reading: _____

_____
_____
_____
_____
_____
_____
_____
_____
_____
_____
_____
_____
_____
_____
_____
_____

Occurrences, Accomplishments & Results: _____

_____
_____
_____
_____
_____
_____
_____
_____
_____
_____
_____
_____
_____
_____
_____
_____
_____
_____
_____

Chakra Divination Ultimate Balance Journal

Today's Date: _____ **Time**: _____
Location: _____
Spread Chosen: _____
Chakra Cards: _____
_____

Problem Cards: _____
_____

Course of Action Cards: _____
_____

Solution Cards: _____
_____

My Initial Thoughts & Plan of Action: _____
_____
_____
_____
_____
_____
_____
_____
_____
_____
_____
_____
_____
_____
_____
_____
_____
_____
_____
_____
_____
_____
_____
_____
_____
_____

Looking Back, Reflections on the Reading: _____

Occurrences, Accomplishments & Results: _____

Chakra Divination Ultimate Balance Journal

Today's Date: _____ **Time**: _____
Location: _____
Spread Chosen: _____
Chakra Cards: _____
_____

Problem Cards:_____
_____

Course of Action Cards:_____
_____

Solution Cards:_____
_____

My Initial Thoughts & Plan of Action: _____
_____
_____
_____
_____
_____
_____
_____
_____
_____
_____
_____
_____
_____
_____
_____
_____
_____
_____
_____
_____
_____
_____
_____
_____
_____

Looking Back, Reflections on the Reading: _____

_____
_____
_____
_____
_____
_____
_____
_____
_____
_____
_____
_____
_____
_____
_____
_____

Occurrences, Accomplishments & Results: _____

_____
_____
_____
_____
_____
_____
_____
_____
_____
_____
_____
_____
_____
_____
_____
_____
_____
_____
_____
_____

Chakra Divination Ultimate Balance Journal

Today's Date: _____ ***Time***: _____
Location: _____
Spread Chosen: _____
Chakra Cards: _____
_____

Problem Cards: _____
_____

Course of Action Cards: _____
_____

Solution Cards: _____
_____

My Initial Thoughts & Plan of Action: _____
_____
_____
_____
_____
_____
_____
_____
_____
_____
_____
_____
_____
_____
_____
_____
_____
_____
_____
_____
_____
_____
_____
_____
_____
_____

Looking Back, Reflections on the Reading: _____

Occurrences, Accomplishments & Results: _____

Chakra Divination Ultimate Balance Journal

Today's Date: _____ **Time**: _____
Location: _____
Spread Chosen: _____
Chakra Cards: _____

Problem Cards:_____

Course of Action Cards:_____

Solution Cards:_____

My Initial Thoughts & Plan of Action: _____
_____
_____
_____
_____
_____
_____
_____
_____
_____
_____
_____
_____
_____
_____
_____
_____
_____
_____
_____
_____
_____
_____
_____
_____
_____
_____

Looking Back, Reflections on the Reading: _____

_____
_____
_____
_____
_____
_____
_____
_____
_____
_____
_____
_____
_____
_____
_____
_____
_____
_____

Occurrences, Accomplishments & Results: _____

_____
_____
_____
_____
_____
_____
_____
_____
_____
_____
_____
_____
_____
_____
_____
_____
_____
_____
_____
_____

Chakra Divination Ultimate Balance Journal

Today's Date: _____ **Time**: _____
Location: _____
Spread Chosen: _____
Chakra Cards: _____

Problem Cards:_____

Course of Action Cards:_____

Solution Cards:_____

My Initial Thoughts & Plan of Action: _____
_____
_____
_____
_____
_____
_____
_____
_____
_____
_____
_____
_____
_____
_____
_____
_____
_____
_____
_____
_____
_____
_____
_____
_____

Looking Back, Reflections on the Reading: _____

_____
_____
_____
_____
_____
_____
_____
_____
_____
_____
_____
_____
_____
_____
_____
_____
_____

Occurrences, Accomplishments & Results: _____

_____
_____
_____
_____
_____
_____
_____
_____
_____
_____
_____
_____
_____
_____
_____
_____
_____
_____
_____
_____

Chakra Divination Ultimate Balance Journal

Today's Date: _____ **Time**: _____
Location: _____
Spread Chosen: _____
Chakra Cards: _____
_____

Problem Cards:_____
_____

Course of Action Cards:_____
_____

Solution Cards:_____
_____

My Initial Thoughts & Plan of Action: _____
_____
_____
_____
_____
_____
_____
_____
_____
_____
_____
_____
_____
_____
_____
_____
_____
_____
_____
_____
_____
_____
_____
_____
_____
_____
_____

Looking Back, Reflections on the Reading: _____

_____

Occurrences, Accomplishments & Results: _____

Chakra Divination Ultimate Balance Journal

Today's Date: _____ *Time*: _____
Location: _____
Spread Chosen: _____
Chakra Cards: _____
_____

Problem Cards:_____
_____

Course of Action Cards:_____
_____

Solution Cards:_____
_____

My Initial Thoughts & Plan of Action: _____
_____
_____
_____
_____
_____
_____
_____
_____
_____
_____
_____
_____
_____
_____
_____
_____
_____
_____
_____
_____
_____
_____
_____
_____
_____
_____

Looking Back, Reflections on the Reading: _____

Occurrences, Accomplishments & Results: _____

Today's Date: _____ *Time*: _____
Location: _____
Spread Chosen: _____
Chakra Cards: _____
_____

Problem Cards:_____
_____

Course of Action Cards:_____
_____

Solution Cards:_____
_____

My Initial Thoughts & Plan of Action: _____
_____
_____
_____
_____
_____
_____
_____
_____
_____
_____
_____
_____
_____
_____
_____
_____
_____
_____
_____
_____
_____
_____
_____
_____

Looking Back, Reflections on the Reading: _____

_____
_____
_____
_____
_____
_____
_____
_____
_____
_____
_____
_____
_____
_____
_____
_____
_____

Occurrences, Accomplishments & Results: _____

_____
_____
_____
_____
_____
_____
_____
_____
_____
_____
_____
_____
_____
_____
_____
_____
_____
_____
_____
_____
_____
_____

Today's Date: _____ *Time*: _____
Location: _____
Spread Chosen: _____
Chakra Cards: _____

Problem Cards:_____

Course of Action Cards:_____

Solution Cards:_____

My Initial Thoughts & Plan of Action: _____
_____
_____
_____
_____
_____
_____
_____
_____
_____
_____
_____
_____
_____
_____
_____
_____
_____
_____
_____
_____
_____
_____
_____
_____
_____

Chakra Divination Ultimate Balance Journal

Looking Back, Reflections on the Reading: _____

_____
_____
_____
_____
_____
_____
_____
_____
_____
_____
_____
_____
_____
_____
_____
_____
_____

Occurrences, Accomplishments & Results: _____

_____
_____
_____
_____
_____
_____
_____
_____
_____
_____
_____
_____
_____
_____
_____
_____
_____
_____
_____
_____

Chakra Divination Ultimate Balance Journal

Today's Date: _____ ***Time***: _____
Location: _____
Spread Chosen: _____
Chakra Cards: _____
_____

Problem Cards: _____
_____

Course of Action Cards: _____
_____

Solution Cards: _____
_____

My Initial Thoughts & Plan of Action: _____
_____
_____
_____
_____
_____
_____
_____
_____
_____
_____
_____
_____
_____
_____
_____
_____
_____
_____
_____
_____
_____
_____
_____
_____
_____

Looking Back, Reflections on the Reading: _____

Occurrences, Accomplishments & Results: _____

Today's Date: _____ *Time*: _____
Location: _____
Spread Chosen: _____
Chakra Cards: _____

Problem Cards: _____

Course of Action Cards: _____

Solution Cards: _____

My Initial Thoughts & Plan of Action: _____
_____
_____
_____
_____
_____
_____
_____
_____
_____
_____
_____
_____
_____
_____
_____
_____
_____
_____
_____
_____
_____
_____
_____
_____
_____
_____

Looking Back, Reflections on the Reading: _____

Occurrences, Accomplishments & Results: _____

Today's Date: _____ ***Time***: _____
Location: _____
Spread Chosen: _____
Chakra Cards: _____
_____

Problem Cards: _____
_____

Course of Action Cards: _____
_____

Solution Cards: _____
_____

My Initial Thoughts & Plan of Action: _____
_____
_____
_____
_____
_____
_____
_____
_____
_____
_____
_____
_____
_____
_____
_____
_____
_____
_____
_____
_____
_____
_____
_____
_____
_____
_____

Looking Back, Reflections on the Reading: _____

Occurrences, Accomplishments & Results: _____

Chakra Divination Ultimate Balance Journal

Today's Date: _____ **Time**: _____
Location: _____
Spread Chosen: _____
Chakra Cards: _____
_____

Problem Cards:_____
_____

Course of Action Cards:_____
_____

Solution Cards:_____
_____

My Initial Thoughts & Plan of Action: _____
_____
_____
_____
_____
_____
_____
_____
_____
_____
_____
_____
_____
_____
_____
_____
_____
_____
_____
_____
_____
_____
_____
_____
_____

Looking Back, Reflections on the Reading: _____

Occurrences, Accomplishments & Results: _____

Today's Date: _____ **Time**: _____
Location: _____
Spread Chosen: _____
Chakra Cards: _____
_____

Problem Cards:_____
_____

Course of Action Cards:_____
_____

Solution Cards:_____
_____

My Initial Thoughts & Plan of Action: _____
_____
_____
_____
_____
_____
_____
_____
_____
_____
_____
_____
_____
_____
_____
_____
_____
_____
_____
_____
_____
_____
_____
_____
_____
_____
_____
_____

Looking Back, Reflections on the Reading: _____

_____
_____
_____
_____
_____
_____
_____
_____
_____
_____
_____
_____
_____
_____
_____
_____
_____
_____

Occurrences, Accomplishments & Results: _____

_____
_____
_____
_____
_____
_____
_____
_____
_____
_____
_____
_____
_____
_____
_____
_____
_____
_____
_____
_____
_____

Today's Date: _____ ***Time***: _____
Location: _____
Spread Chosen: _____
Chakra Cards: _____
_____

Problem Cards:_____
_____

Course of Action Cards:_____
_____

Solution Cards:_____
_____

My Initial Thoughts & Plan of Action: _____
_____
_____
_____
_____
_____
_____
_____
_____
_____
_____
_____
_____
_____
_____
_____
_____
_____
_____
_____
_____
_____
_____
_____
_____
_____

Looking Back, Reflections on the Reading: _____

_____
_____
_____
_____
_____
_____
_____
_____
_____
_____
_____
_____
_____
_____
_____

Occurrences, Accomplishments & Results: _____

_____
_____
_____
_____
_____
_____
_____
_____
_____
_____
_____
_____
_____
_____
_____
_____
_____
_____
_____

Chakra Divination Ultimate Balance Journal

Today's Date: _____ ***Time***: _____
Location: _____
Spread Chosen: _____
Chakra Cards: _____

Problem Cards:_____

Course of Action Cards:_____

Solution Cards:_____

My Initial Thoughts & Plan of Action: _____
_____
_____
_____
_____
_____
_____
_____
_____
_____
_____
_____
_____
_____
_____
_____
_____
_____
_____
_____
_____
_____
_____
_____
_____

Looking Back, Reflections on the Reading: _____

_____
_____
_____
_____
_____
_____
_____
_____
_____
_____
_____
_____
_____
_____
_____

Occurrences, Accomplishments & Results: _____

_____
_____
_____
_____
_____
_____
_____
_____
_____
_____
_____
_____
_____
_____
_____
_____
_____
_____

Today's Date: _____ **Time**: _____
Location: _____
Spread Chosen: _____
Chakra Cards: _____
_____

Problem Cards:_____
_____

Course of Action Cards:_____
_____

Solution Cards:_____
_____

My Initial Thoughts & Plan of Action: _____
_____
_____
_____
_____
_____
_____
_____
_____
_____
_____
_____
_____
_____
_____
_____
_____
_____
_____
_____
_____
_____
_____
_____
_____

Looking Back, Reflections on the Reading: _____

Occurrences, Accomplishments & Results: _____

Chakra Divination Ultimate Balance Journal

Today's Date: _____ **Time**: _____
Location: _____
Spread Chosen: _____
Chakra Cards: _____
_____

Problem Cards:_____
_____

Course of Action Cards:_____
_____

Solution Cards:_____
_____

My Initial Thoughts & Plan of Action: _____
_____
_____
_____
_____
_____
_____
_____
_____
_____
_____
_____
_____
_____
_____
_____
_____
_____
_____
_____
_____
_____
_____
_____
_____

Looking Back, Reflections on the Reading: _____

_____
_____
_____
_____
_____
_____
_____
_____
_____
_____
_____
_____
_____
_____
_____
_____

Occurrences, Accomplishments & Results: _____

_____
_____
_____
_____
_____
_____
_____
_____
_____
_____
_____
_____
_____
_____
_____
_____
_____
_____
_____

Today's Date: _____ **Time**: _____
Location: _____
Spread Chosen: _____
Chakra Cards: _____
_____

Problem Cards:_____
_____

Course of Action Cards:_____
_____

Solution Cards:_____
_____

My Initial Thoughts & Plan of Action: _____
_____
_____
_____
_____
_____
_____
_____
_____
_____
_____
_____
_____
_____
_____
_____
_____
_____
_____
_____
_____
_____
_____
_____
_____
_____

Looking Back, Reflections on the Reading: _____

_____

Occurrences, Accomplishments & Results: _____

_____

Today's Date: _____ *Time*: _____
Location: _____
Spread Chosen: _____
Chakra Cards: _____
_____

Problem Cards:_____
_____

Course of Action Cards:_____
_____

Solution Cards:_____
_____

My Initial Thoughts & Plan of Action: _____

Looking Back, Reflections on the Reading: _____

_____
_____
_____
_____
_____
_____
_____
_____
_____
_____
_____
_____
_____
_____
_____

Occurrences, Accomplishments & Results: _____

_____
_____
_____
_____
_____
_____
_____
_____
_____
_____
_____
_____
_____
_____
_____
_____
_____
_____
_____
_____

Today's Date: _____ *Time*: _____
Location: _____
Spread Chosen: _____
Chakra Cards: _____
_____

Problem Cards:_____
_____

Course of Action Cards:_____
_____

Solution Cards:_____
_____

My Initial Thoughts & Plan of Action: _____
_____
_____
_____
_____
_____
_____
_____
_____
_____
_____
_____
_____
_____
_____
_____
_____
_____
_____
_____
_____
_____
_____
_____
_____
_____
_____

Looking Back, Reflections on the Reading: _____

_____
_____
_____
_____
_____
_____
_____
_____
_____
_____
_____
_____
_____
_____
_____
_____

Occurrences, Accomplishments & Results: _____

_____
_____
_____
_____
_____
_____
_____
_____
_____
_____
_____
_____
_____
_____
_____
_____
_____
_____
_____
_____

Chakra Divination Ultimate Balance Journal

Today's Date: _____ ***Time***: _____
Location: _____
Spread Chosen: _____
Chakra Cards: _____

Problem Cards: _____
_____

Course of Action Cards: _____
_____

Solution Cards: _____
_____

My Initial Thoughts & Plan of Action: _____
_____
_____
_____
_____
_____
_____
_____
_____
_____
_____
_____
_____
_____
_____
_____
_____
_____
_____
_____
_____
_____
_____
_____
_____

Looking Back, Reflections on the Reading: _____

Occurrences, Accomplishments & Results: _____

Chakra Divination Ultimate Balance Journal

Today's Date: _____ **Time**: _____
Location: _____
Spread Chosen: _____
Chakra Cards: _____
_____

Problem Cards: _____
_____

Course of Action Cards: _____
_____

Solution Cards: _____
_____

My Initial Thoughts & Plan of Action: _____
_____
_____
_____
_____
_____
_____
_____
_____
_____
_____
_____
_____
_____
_____
_____
_____
_____
_____
_____
_____
_____
_____
_____
_____
_____
_____
_____

Looking Back, Reflections on the Reading: _____

Occurrences, Accomplishments & Results: _____

Today's Date: _____ *Time*: _____
Location: _____
Spread Chosen: _____
Chakra Cards: _____
_____

Problem Cards:_____
_____

Course of Action Cards:_____
_____

Solution Cards:_____
_____

My Initial Thoughts & Plan of Action: _____
_____
_____
_____
_____
_____
_____
_____
_____
_____
_____
_____
_____
_____
_____
_____
_____
_____
_____
_____
_____
_____
_____
_____
_____
_____

Looking Back, Reflections on the Reading: _____

_____
_____
_____
_____
_____
_____
_____
_____
_____
_____
_____
_____
_____
_____

Occurrences, Accomplishments & Results: _____

_____
_____
_____
_____
_____
_____
_____
_____
_____
_____
_____
_____
_____
_____
_____
_____
_____
_____

Chakra Divination Ultimate Balance Journal

Today's Date: _____ ***Time***: _____
Location: _____
Spread Chosen: _____
Chakra Cards: _____

Problem Cards:_____

Course of Action Cards:_____

Solution Cards:_____

My Initial Thoughts & Plan of Action: _____
_____
_____
_____
_____
_____
_____
_____
_____
_____
_____
_____
_____
_____
_____
_____
_____
_____
_____
_____
_____
_____
_____
_____
_____
_____
_____

Looking Back, Reflections on the Reading: _____

Occurrences, Accomplishments & Results: _____

Today's Date: _____ ***Time***: _____

Location: _____

Spread Chosen: _____

Chakra Cards: _____
_____

Problem Cards:_____
_____

Course of Action Cards:_____
_____

Solution Cards:_____
_____

My Initial Thoughts & Plan of Action: _____
_____
_____
_____
_____
_____
_____
_____
_____
_____
_____
_____
_____
_____
_____
_____
_____
_____
_____
_____
_____
_____
_____
_____
_____
_____
_____

Looking Back, Reflections on the Reading: _____

Occurrences, Accomplishments & Results: _____

Chakra Divination Ultimate Balance Journal

Today's Date: _____ ***Time***: _____
Location: _____
Spread Chosen: _____
Chakra Cards: _____

Problem Cards:_____

Course of Action Cards:_____

Solution Cards:_____

My Initial Thoughts & Plan of Action: _____
_____
_____
_____
_____
_____
_____
_____
_____
_____
_____
_____
_____
_____
_____
_____
_____
_____
_____
_____
_____
_____
_____
_____
_____

Looking Back, Reflections on the Reading: _____

_____
_____
_____
_____
_____
_____
_____
_____
_____
_____
_____
_____
_____
_____
_____

Occurrences, Accomplishments & Results: _____

_____
_____
_____
_____
_____
_____
_____
_____
_____
_____
_____
_____
_____
_____
_____
_____
_____
_____
_____

Chakra Divination Ultimate Balance Journal

Today's Date: _____ **Time**: _____
Location: _____
Spread Chosen: _____
Chakra Cards: _____

Problem Cards: _____

Course of Action Cards: _____

Solution Cards: _____

My Initial Thoughts & Plan of Action: _____
_____
_____
_____
_____
_____
_____
_____
_____
_____
_____
_____
_____
_____
_____
_____
_____
_____
_____
_____
_____
_____
_____
_____
_____

Looking Back, Reflections on the Reading: _____

_____
_____
_____
_____
_____
_____
_____
_____
_____
_____
_____
_____
_____
_____
_____

Occurrences, Accomplishments & Results: _____

_____
_____
_____
_____
_____
_____
_____
_____
_____
_____
_____
_____
_____
_____
_____
_____
_____
_____
_____
_____

Today's Date: _____ **Time**: _____
Location: _____
Spread Chosen: _____
Chakra Cards: _____
_____

Problem Cards: _____
_____

Course of Action Cards: _____
_____

Solution Cards: _____
_____

My Initial Thoughts & Plan of Action: _____
_____
_____
_____
_____
_____
_____
_____
_____
_____
_____
_____
_____
_____
_____
_____
_____
_____
_____
_____
_____
_____
_____
_____
_____
_____
_____
_____

Looking Back, Reflections on the Reading: _____

Occurrences, Accomplishments & Results: _____

Today's Date: _____ *Time*: _____
Location: _____
Spread Chosen: _____
Chakra Cards: _____

Problem Cards:_____

Course of Action Cards:_____

Solution Cards:_____

My Initial Thoughts & Plan of Action: _____
_____
_____
_____
_____
_____
_____
_____
_____
_____
_____
_____
_____
_____
_____
_____
_____
_____
_____
_____
_____
_____
_____
_____
_____
_____
_____

Looking Back, Reflections on the Reading: _____

Occurrences, Accomplishments & Results: _____

Today's Date: _____ *Time*: _____
Location: _____
Spread Chosen: _____
Chakra Cards: _____

Problem Cards:_____

Course of Action Cards:_____

Solution Cards:_____

My Initial Thoughts & Plan of Action: _____
_____
_____
_____
_____
_____
_____
_____
_____
_____
_____
_____
_____
_____
_____
_____
_____
_____
_____
_____
_____
_____
_____
_____
_____
_____
_____

Looking Back, Reflections on the Reading: _____

_____
_____
_____
_____
_____
_____
_____
_____
_____
_____
_____
_____
_____
_____
_____
_____

Occurrences, Accomplishments & Results: _____

_____
_____
_____
_____
_____
_____
_____
_____
_____
_____
_____
_____
_____
_____
_____
_____
_____
_____
_____
_____

Today's Date: _____ **Time**: _____
Location: _____
Spread Chosen: _____
Chakra Cards: _____
_____

Problem Cards: _____
_____

Course of Action Cards: _____
_____

Solution Cards: _____
_____

My Initial Thoughts & Plan of Action: _____
_____
_____
_____
_____
_____
_____
_____
_____
_____
_____
_____
_____
_____
_____
_____
_____
_____
_____
_____
_____
_____
_____
_____
_____
_____
_____
_____

Looking Back, Reflections on the Reading: _____

Occurrences, Accomplishments & Results: _____

Today's Date: _____ **Time**: _____
Location: _____
Spread Chosen: _____
Chakra Cards: _____
_____

Problem Cards: _____
_____

Course of Action Cards: _____
_____

Solution Cards: _____
_____

My Initial Thoughts & Plan of Action: _____
_____
_____
_____
_____
_____
_____
_____
_____
_____
_____
_____
_____
_____
_____
_____
_____
_____
_____
_____
_____
_____
_____
_____
_____
_____
_____

Looking Back, Reflections on the Reading: _____

_____
_____
_____
_____
_____
_____
_____
_____
_____
_____
_____
_____
_____
_____
_____
_____

Occurrences, Accomplishments & Results: _____

_____
_____
_____
_____
_____
_____
_____
_____
_____
_____
_____
_____
_____
_____
_____
_____
_____
_____
_____

VISIT MELISSA ALVAREZ ONLINE AT
www.ChakraDivination.com
www.MelissaA.com
www.APsychicHaven.com
Email Melissa at contact@chakradivination.com

www.ingramcontent.com/pod-product-compliance
Lightning Source LLC
Chambersburg PA
CBHW060520100426
42743CB00009B/1386